COLONIAL PEOPLE

# The Glassblower

## CHRISTINE PETERSEN

 **Marshall Cavendish**
Benchmark
New York

This publication represents the opinions and views of the author based on Christine Petersen's personal experience, knowledge,
and research. The information in this book serves as a general guide only. The author and publisher have used their best efforts
in preparing this book and disclaim liability rising directly and indirectly from the use and application of this book.

Other Marshall Cavendish Offices:

Marshall Cavendish International (Asia) Private Limited, 1 New Industrial Road, Singapore 536196 • Marshall Cavendish
International (Thailand) Co Ltd., 253 Asoke, 12th Flr, Sukhumvit 21 Road, Klongtoey Nua, Wattana, Bangkok 10110,
Thailand • Marshall Cavendish (Malaysia) Sdn Bhd, Times Subang, Lot 46, Subang Hi-Tech Industrial Park, Batu Tiga,
40000 Shah Alam, Selangor Darul Ehsan, Malaysia

Marshall Cavendish is a trademark of Times Publishing Limited

All websites were available and accurate when this book was sent to press.

Library of Congress Cataloging-in-Publication Data

Petersen, Christine.
The glassblower / Christine Petersen.
p. cm. — (Colonial people)
Summary: "Explore the life of a colonial glassblower and his importance to
the community, as well as everyday life, responsibilities, and social
practices during that time"— Provided by publisher.
Includes index.
ISBN 978-1-60870-413-2 (print)
ISBN 978-1-60870-637-2 (ebook)
1. Glass blowing and working—United States—History—Colonial period, ca.
1600-1775. 2. Glassworkers—United States—Social conditions—17th century.
3. Glassworkers—United States—Social conditions—18th century. I. Title.

TP859.P48 2012
666'.122097309033—dc22
2010033901

Editor: Joy Bean
Publisher: Michelle Bisson
Art Director: Anahid Hamparian
Series Designer: Kay Petronio

Expert Reader: Paul Douglas Newman, Ph.D., Department of History, University of Pittsburgh at Johnstown

Photo research by Marybeth Kavanagh

Cover photo by Private Collection/Archives Charmet/The Bridgeman Art Library

The photographs in this book are used by permission and through the courtesy of: *Alamy*: ClassicStock, 4; David Stuckel, 13;
M. Timothy O'Keefe, 25; INTERFOTO, 31; *The Art Archive*: Museo Vetrario Murano/Dagli Orti, 7; Museum of Decorative
Arts Prague/Alfredo Dagli Orti, 24; *The Image Works*: AAAC/TopFoto, 8; Museum of London / HIP, 23; Peter Hvizdak, 29;
*Getty Images*: MPI, 10; *North Wind Picture Archives*: 16, 17; *Photo Researchers Inc.*: 19; *The Colonial Williamsburg Foundation*, 35;
*Art Directors*: Constance Toms, 37; *The Granger Collection, New York*, 40

Printed in Malaysia (T)
1 3 5 6 4 2

# CONTENTS

# ONE

## Industry in the New World

The sixteenth century was an era of discovery for the powerful nations of Europe. Spain, Portugal, the Netherlands, and France sent explorers around the world in search of treasure and new markets in which to buy and sell goods. Each of these nations set up bases in the New World—on the continents of South or North America and among the islands of the Caribbean Sea.

England's queen, Elizabeth I, could not resist an opportunity to compete with her neighboring countries. In 1585 she sent sailors in search of a suitable location for an English colony in the New World. Her representatives crossed the Atlantic Ocean and sailed along North America's eastern shoreline. They claimed a long stretch of coastal land for the queen and called it Virginia.

*The first English explorers and settlers came to North America in small, wooden sailing ships similar to this one.*

# A Vision for Virginia

Attempts to settle Virginia in the 1580s failed. The first colonists were unprepared for this distant land, where life was so much harder than it was in England. The earliest Virginians did not plant enough food, and they never formed a trusting relationship with local American Indians. But the idea of colonization continued to tempt English merchants. They saw Virginia as a source of useful materials that could be sold in England, from gold and furs to medicinal plants and exotic birds for the pet trade. Wood was another resource readily available in Virginia. This was very different from England, whose forests had been cut down decades earlier. Important English industries such as shipbuilding and cabinetmaking required wood and would pay well for it.

Merchants also hoped that Virginia could provide materials to start profitable industries such as glassmaking. At this time the English usually **imported** fine glass from Italy and other parts of Europe. During the mid-sixteenth century, people developed new techniques for making glass. As a greater variety of glass objects became available, the demand for glass began to increase. Wealthy English families were willing to pay for luxuries such as glass windowpanes. They wanted to drink from wineglasses and tumblers instead of leather or wooden cups like the common people. The British equally valued **tableware,** as glass dishes, bowls, and pitchers added sparkle to meals and showed off a family's position in society.

To compete with European imports, the English started a small glassmaking industry. But the nation's appetite for glass was huge, and a few glassblowers could not satisfy it. Glass produced in the Virginia Colony would be quite valuable.

*Seventeenth-century glassmakers produced a variety of elegant objects, such as wineglasses, which graced the tables of wealthy colonists.*

# An Ancient Art

Human beings first manufactured glass in Mesopotamia, in the area surrounding the great Tigris and Euphrates rivers. (This region is presently home to the countries of Iraq and Syria.) Mesopotamian glassblowers began to make vases and other items more than 4,500 years ago. The first written record of their work dates to 1,500 bce, around the same time that Egyptians began glassmaking. Glass found in ancient Mesopotamian ruins is complex and beautiful, with many colors and patterns. Greek and Roman craftsmen took up glassblowing in later centuries. By the eighth century ce, people in Asia were also producing glass.

Very few craftsmen could do this complex work, so they were held in the highest honor. From the fifteenth century onward, Italy was recognized as the heart of glassmaking in Europe. Glass made in Germany or Bohemia (a region that is now part of the Czech Republic) came in at a close second place for quality. This glass was clear rather than colored, and it was sturdier than Italian glass. Craftsmen could carve or etch the glass to produce marvelous designs.

# Hard Times in a New Land

Failed efforts had shown that colonizing Virginia would be challenging and expensive. In 1606 a group of merchants decided to share the costs of creating a settlement there. With the approval of King James I, the merchants formed a business on a piece of land in southern Virginia. They called it the Virginia Company of London. Soon the company had gathered supplies, ships, and men to make the long journey.

In late April 1607 the Virginia Company's three ships sailed into Chesapeake Bay on the central Atlantic Coast of America. On board were the crew and 104 settlers, all men. Recognizing Spanish pirates as the new colony's greatest threat, the company had recommended settling inland rather than along the coastline. The ship captains continued up the nearest large river until they found a peninsula surrounded by water that was deep enough to dock in. There the men established a tent camp. Within a few weeks they had built a triangular fort. Although most of the original settlers expected to make their fortunes and return to England, this fort would become the first permanent English settlement in America. The men called it Jamestown in honor of their king.

The company had chosen a large number of gentlemen to join the group. The men were used to being leaders, not workers, and

*The original Jamestown settlers built a triangular fort to protect their homes and supplies.*

they were reluctant to help with the work of building the colony. The other settlers were craftsmen, laborers, and soldiers who had some useful skills. None of the men had ever been farmers, however. Rather than learning this important skill, they set out to find gold and other valuable resources. Since most of the men expected to return to England, it seemed foolish to spend time building and planting.

By midsummer the food supplies the men had brought on the ship began to run low, and the men had to **ration** what was left. Many began to fall ill, and some died. The settlers had naively placed Jamestown in the middle of a swamp. It was infested with mosquitoes that carried disease, and the drinking water was tainted with salt. The men traded with the local Powhatan Indians for corn and meat. Without this food, the men might not have survived until supply ships arrived in the winter and fall of 1608.

## The Jamestown Glasshouse

Two supply expeditions from England brought more settlers to Jamestown. The second expedition, which contained eight men from Germany and Poland, was especially important to the Virginia Company. The company had hired these men to start Jamestown's first industries. One of the new workers' assignments was to make pitch and tar, sticky liquids cooked from pine tree sap used to waterproof ships. They were also charged with producing **potash** from the ashes of burned wood, for use in soap making. The Virginia Company could sell these three products in England. Some of the potash would remain in Jamestown, where the settlers would use it to make glass.

The German and Polish men were experienced glassmakers, and they had brought their equipment with them. Their gear included massive pots called **crucibles**, which were shaped from heat-resistant clay. The Virginia Company built the craftsmen a **glasshouse** in the woods just inland of the Jamestown settlement. Measuring 37 feet by 50 feet (11.3 by 15.2 meters), this factory held brick furnaces that melted glass.

All the other glassmaking materials were available around Jamestown. The forest supplied wood for potash and furnace fuel. Workers collected sand from the riverbank. The Chesapeake Bay provided seaweed and oyster shells. The glassblowers burned seaweed to make **soda ash**, and they crushed oyster shells before burning them to produce **lime**. Mixed together, these ingredients were called **frit**. Glassmakers transferred the frit to a large furnace to be melted. Then they used a long pipe to collect blobs of the resulting gooey, burning-hot liquid. A glassblower blew air into this blob to form a bubble, which he could shape into any number of useful objects. The Jamestown glassblowers made small numbers of windowpanes, bottles, and cups. The finished glass was transparent, with a green tint.

In winter 1609, starvation and bitter cold struck the region. More than four hundred colonists died or ran away to live in

*The ingredients for glass were melted in a huge furnace made from river stones or clay bricks.*

Powhatan Indian villages. All but sixty-five Jamestown colonists died. None of the glassblowers survived.

Merchants of the Virginia Company learned that American Indians found glass just as tempting as their fellow English colonists did. Indians believed that shiny objects could attract the spirits of their ancestors. In 1622 the merchants brought several Italian glassblowers to the colony. The new arrivals' job was to make a large supply of glass beads to trade with tribes around Jamestown. The Italians survived an Indian raid in which almost half the colonists were killed, but the craftsmen became ill and died soon afterward. At that point, the Virginia Company gave up its efforts at glassmaking. Colonists continued to crave glass, however, and talented glassblowers eventually found ways to pursue their craft in the expanding colonies.

# TWO

## The Glassblower's Challenge

Despite the difficulties of life in the New World, colonists continued to arrive in the decades following the establishment of Jamestown. By 1732 England possessed thirteen colonies along the Atlantic coastline. Colonial Americans learned to farm and became skilled at making many of the items they needed in order to survive.

Colonial communities had a wide variety of craftsmen. Most villages had a local blacksmith who forged iron and steel tools. A tanner produced leather, which the shoemaker and tailor made into clothing. An apothecary provided medicines, and a miller ground grain for families and bakers to use to make bread. These goods and services made life easier for everyone. By contrast, glass was a luxury item that many colonists could not afford. As a result, glassblowers struggled to find a place in colonial

*Blacksmiths were part of the community in which the glassblower worked.*

society. But their work provided a touch of beauty that everyone could appreciate. And persistence paid off. As colonial populations increased, so did the demand for glass.

## Who Can Pay the Price?

In the seventeenth century, most colonial Americans lived as their ancestors had lived for generations. Rather than buying windowpanes, they installed oiled paper or sliding wooden frames in their windows to keep out bad weather and animals. Lamp oil and candles were almost as rare and costly as the glass lamps and candlesticks used to hold them. To solve the problem of light, early Americans rose with the sun and went to bed at sunset. At the dinner table, they rarely used fancy plates, glasses, or serving dishes. Instead, they put their food on wooden plates or in baskets. Because local water supplies were often polluted with trash and sewage, colonists had little access to clean drinking water. Commoners drank weak beer with every meal. They stored the ale in wooden casks and served it in leather or wooden mugs.

A glassblower's main customers were wealthy colonists who wanted to live like their equals in England. They eagerly imported glass windowpanes from England and Europe to adorn their homes. The wealthy also wanted bottles of wine to serve at meals and ornate glasses in which to drink it. They ordered decorative vases, pitchers, serving dishes, chandeliers, and many more glass objects. Many people faced disappointment when their prized glass goods arrived. The fragile items often shattered during the long ocean voyage. When merchants lost part of their shipment, they charged extra for unbroken items to make up for the loss. This added significantly to the price of imported glass. The colonial glassblower's best hope for success was to provide some of these goods at a lower price than English importers did.

*Common people could not afford glass, so they drank from carved wooden mugs.*

## Old Recipes, New Techniques

The members of the Virginia Company had believed it would be easy to make glass in America. This turned out to be a misconception for several reasons. England was home to millions of people, including many craftsmen. But there were very few glassblowers, and they refused to leave successful factories in their home country to set up new ones in the colonies. Almost all colonial glassblowers came from countries in mainland Europe. Immigrants from these nations established their own small communities within the English colonies, though they never made up a large part of the population.

Once a glassblower made it to the colonies, he needed a very particular set of supplies. He might have brought his glassblowing tools from home. If not, he could have a local blacksmith make them. His neighbors might help construct the glasshouse. But no one could make glass without clay, which was used to make crucibles and to build furnaces. The glassblower needed a special type of clay that did not crack when it dried and could withstand extreme heat. It took the colonists many decades to find this type of clay locally. Until then they had to import it. English glassblowers had access to an excellent source of clay in central England, but they did not want to share it.

# Meet the Colonial Glassblowers

We know very little about the earliest colonial glassblowers. Among them were German immigrants who settled in Salem, Massachusetts. Their glasshouse opened in 1638 and remained productive for more than thirty years. In the 1650s glassmakers Jan Smeedes and Evert Duyckinck established competing factories in the Dutch colony of New Amsterdam (which later became New York under English rule).

The stars of colonial glassmaking appeared in the mid-eighteenth century. German-born Caspar Wistar settled in Salem County, New Jersey, in 1717. After becoming wealthy as a maker of brass buttons, he decided to build a glasshouse. In 1739 Wistar hired Dutch glassmakers to run his factory and to teach him their craft. He began making simple windowpanes and bottles, and within a few years he was producing lovely objects in a variety of styles and colors. Benjamin Franklin ordered glass tubes from Wistar to use in his experiments on electricity. Until 1780 Wistar's factory also made glass lamps, serving pitchers, cruet bottles to hold condiments, and many more items.

*Ben Franklin and other early scientists sometimes used glass containers to conduct experiments.*

Even if all the materials were ready to go, early colonial glassblowers still faced problems when they tried to produce a batch of glass. The ingredients did not melt. Jamestown colonist George Sandys described this situation as early as 1623. Jamestown's Italian glassblowers had built a typical fire in their furnace, but the ingredients in their crucible would not turn to liquid. "The fire hath now beene six weeks in ye furnace, and yet nothinge effected," wrote Sandys. "They complain that the sand will not run. . . ." Colonial glassblowers found this challenge frustrating. Why didn't their time-proven techniques work in America?

They had to be creative and patient to solve this mystery. Glassblowers were used to mixing sand, potash, soda ash, and lime in specific proportions and heating the furnace to a particular temperature to melt them. The key was experimentation. The craftsmen made slight changes in the furnace temperature and adjusted the balance of ingredients. Sand seemed to be the most crucial factor, as some types melted better than others. Eventually glassblowers found the right conditions and produced solid, useful glass to sell in their communities.

# THREE

## In the Glasshouse

It was not unusual for colonial craftsmen to perform their jobs in an extra room in their homes. If their work was particularly messy, they might build a workshop nearby. Some kept shops to sell their wares. But few craftsmen required a factory as large as the glassblower's.

### The Furnace

At the heart of a glasshouse were the great furnaces, which were kept blazing day and night. The first furnaces, such as those at Jamestown, were made of river stones. Later glassmakers crushed up bits of old crucibles and made the powder into bricks, which retained the fire-resistant quality of the crucible clay. Some furnaces were dome shaped, while others were rectangular. Furnaces could be as large as an entire room in a regular house.

Several smaller furnaces served different purposes during the stages of glassmaking. The craftsman used a fritting furnace to make lime, potash, and soda ash. When these ingredients were ready, the glassmaker mixed them with sand inside the fritting oven and warmed them up for a while. Then he transferred the frit, scoop by scoop, into crucibles in the large main furnace.

The key to successfully melting the frit was extreme heat. Temperatures inside the main furnace sometimes reached 3,000 degrees Fahrenheit (1,650 degrees Celsius). As the frit softened, the glassblower stirred it with a long-handled iron spoon and used a forklike skimmer to collect any solid material that floated to the surface. If not removed, these materials would create imperfections in the glass and alter its color.

It took tremendous amounts of wood to maintain such intense fires. The glassblower usually started the fires weeks before he planned to begin making glass, so the furnace would gradually reach the proper temperature. He also placed crucibles inside the furnace beforehand to warm them up slowly. This reduced the amount of breakage, but the extreme heat always wore down the pots. High temperatures also caused the furnaces to break down. They had to be repaired or rebuilt every couple of years.

*Fires burned constantly to keep temperatures high in the glasshouse's massive fritting furnace.*

Each furnace had a door large enough to fit men and crucibles. It took several workers to lift and move the heavy pots, which they placed beneath windows behind the furnace walls. The glassblower closed the furnace door after he placed

# Shine On

Glassblowing was already an ancient art by the colonial era, but craftsmen were always trying out new styles and methods. In the 1670s a respected English glassmaker named George Ravenscroft began to produce flint glass. He used sand containing flint, which is a dark, shiny rock. Ravenscroft's frit included lead, a metallic chemical that helped the other ingredients melt and mix together more smoothly. People prized flint glass for its remarkable brilliance, which earned it the nickname "crystal glass."

In 1770 the German glassmaker Henry William Stiegel opened a new glasshouse near Philadelphia, Pennsylvania, and called it the American Flint Glassworks. He was proud to be the first colonial glassblower to make this type of glass. Stiegel advertised his products as "equal in beauty and quality to the generality of Flint Glass imported from England." Stiegel spent money faster than he made it, however, and soon went bankrupt. His glasshouse closed after just four years.

the crucibles inside, and the door remained shut anytime the furnace was running.

Attached to the main furnace was a long, slender oven called a **lehr**. The glassblower placed his finished work on trays and slid them into one end of this tunnel-like oven. Heat from the main furnace flowed into this side of the lehr. Workers with metal rods slowly pulled the trays toward the far end, which was cool. This step of **annealing**, or slow cooling, was as important as any other in the glassmaking process. Glass becomes slightly

*Rods were used to push trays of newly made glass through the lehr in order to protect the glassworker's skin from burns.*

smaller as it cools. The surface of the glass loses heat first, and the thicker middle sections follow. If glass cools rapidly, weak points form between these two sections, and the glass breaks easily. The colonial glassblower's lehr allowed glass to cool and solidify slowly, so it could be durable as well as beautiful.

## The Crucial Crucible

The fourth furnace in the glasshouse was a **kiln**, used exclusively for making crucibles. The kiln was often located away from the main furnace, in a separate building or room. When possible, craftsmen called **potters** oversaw the long and tedious process of making crucibles. First, the craftsmen had to order the clay from Europe. When the massive blocks arrived, potters chopped and pounded the clay into tiny fragments, which were left outside to soften and to absorb water. After a year, workers added fragments of old clay pots or furnace bricks to the original clay. Although it was painful, the best way to combine the clay and solid fragments was to squish them together with bare feet. Then the mixture was left outside again. Half a year later, the clay was ready to be molded into crucibles.

The heavy clay had to be shaped in stages. Workers took a block of clay and cut it, then pounded it flat. This formed the crucible's round base. Then the workers laid thick rolls of clay around the edges of the base and stacked them atop each other. As they pressed the rolls together, the walls of the crucible slowly took shape. A crucible could hold as much as 1,300 pounds (590 kilograms) of frit or liquid glass.

Potters needed weeks to mold one crucible—but even then, the big pot was incomplete. It still had to dry in the warm air of the glasshouse for six months to a year. Then the glassblower could carefully place the crucible into the kiln. Although temperatures inside the kiln were lower than those in the main furnace, they were hot enough to remove the last of the water from the clay so it would harden. When it cooled, the crucible was ready for use. By this point, more than two years had gone by since the clay had arrived. In a few months the crucible would break, and a potter would use its fragments to make new pots or furnace bricks. This was part of the cycle that reduced waste in the glasshouse.

# FOUR
## Making Glass

The success of a glasshouse depended on more than the skill of its workers. Glassblowing was a team effort that required cooperation and timing among many men who worked together in close and dangerous conditions.

Glassblowers gained their skills through years of experience that began when they were boys. Through **apprenticeship**, a common form of training in colonial America, craftsmen passed on their skills from generation to generation. In most crafts, a master advertised his need for an apprentice, or a father requested a position for his son. But glassmakers were reluctant to share their knowledge with outsiders. A glassblower's apprentice was often his own son or the son of another man in his shop.

An apprentice started by doing small tasks, such as cleaning the glasshouse and chopping wood. The glassblowers had to be sure they could trust the boy near the hot furnaces and fragile glass. He watched them work, and in time he earned more responsibility. The glassblowers taught him to make potash, soda ash, and lime. He learned to maintain the furnaces and to stoke each fire to just the right temperature. Eventually he joined the men who handled hot glass as it was being shaped into marvelous objects.

Slowly but surely, the apprentice became familiar with the techniques required to produce every item of glass made in the shop, from simple windowpanes to molded bottles and ornate tableware. In return for his training, the apprentice was expected to behave well and to work hard, often six days a week. After a few years he was ready to take an equal place among the men in the glasshouse.

*An apprentice stands ready to cut a ball of hot glass from the blowing rod once it is inside a metal mold.*

## Working as a Team

When the glassworkers were ready to begin making an object, each man took his assigned position. The first worker picked up a **blowing rod**, a metal tube about 5 feet (1.5 m) in length. Because the metal became very hot when it was in contact with liquid glass, one end of the rod was covered with wood. The worker held the wood-covered side and dipped the other into a crucible in the main furnace. As he stirred the material inside the crucible, a mass of hot, liquid glass—called the **parison**—stuck to the blowing rod. The worker lifted the rod out of the furnace and passed it to the next man, who carried it to the blower stationed at a nearby table called the **marver**. The blower puffed air through the blowing rod to form a bubble inside the parison. It took all the power his lungs could produce to make the thick, gooey glass expand. Between puffs the glassblower rolled the bubble on the marver to smooth its sides until it had exactly the size and shape he desired. Now and then he passed the blowing rod back to the first man, who briefly reheated the glass to keep it from solidifying.

If the workers were making window glass, an apprentice brought over a slightly shorter iron rod called a **punty**. He used the punty to pick up a small amount of hot glass from the furnace and pushed it against the end of the bubble. The punty and bubble stuck together. Another worker ran a heated metal knife around the edge of the bubble to cut it free from the blowing rod. Next, the blower balanced the punty on a V-shaped frame in front of the furnace and spun it steadily around. The bubble began to grow longer. Then it flattened out like a wide pancake. When it annealed, this glass disk would be cut into smaller panes. The workers fit the panes together like puzzle pieces and held them together with strips of lead to form a customized windowpane.

*As a worker blows air to expand a parison of hot glass, an apprentice places his punty in the furnace.*

# Test the Power of Water Lamps

While glassblowers often made products for use in the home, some colonial craftsmen also found glass helpful in their work. Lace makers and shoemakers did finely detailed sewing. Because they had no overhead lights, it was sometimes hard for them to see while making small stitches, especially on overcast days. For these craftsmen the glassblower provided globe-shaped lamps. The user filled the bowl with clean water and put a cork or stopper in the narrow neck of the lamp. Then he tipped the neck into a wooden or glass stand, with the globe resting atop it. He placed a lit candle next to the globe and sat on the opposite side. Light from the candle became brighter as it bent through the water and glass of the globe. Glassblowers could increase the amount of light created by changing the shape and size of the globe.

For this activity, try making bright light with different water-filled glass containers to see which one works best. You'll be using a lit candle, so ask an adult to supervise you.

## You Will Need

- 4 to 5 glass containers of different widths and shapes—drinking glasses, storage jars, vases, and so on (they should all have flat surfaces)
- water
- a taper candle
- matches or a lighter
- a rectangular table or other flat workspace in a dimly lit room
- pencil and paper
- ruler (optional)

## Instructions

1. Choose a room with a large table or counter. Make sure you can dim the light in the room by turning down electric lights or drawing the window shades.

2. Fill each container with water.

3. Place the containers in a line on a short end of the table. Leave a little space between each "lamp."

4. Light the candle and hold it a few inches behind the first container. A beam of light will appear on the other side of the lamp and spill across the table. Notice the shape of this beam. How wide and long is it? (If you choose, have your adult helper hold the candle. Use the ruler to take measurements of the beam.) Does the beam change when you move the candle up or down, right or left? Make notes about your observations.

5. Repeat step 4 for each of the remaining containers.

6. Observe what happens when you group the containers together and shine the light through them all.

7. Compare the results. Which single container produced the brightest light? If you were a glassblower, what type of lamp would you design to provide light for hardworking craftsmen?

## The Gaffer's Gift

Window glass was one of the most commonly requested items for a colonial American glassblower. But glassmakers were equally proud of their ability to produce useful and lovely glass objects for other parts of the house. Many of these objects required craftsmen to shape blown glass very carefully. After the blowing process, the workers turned over the punty to the glasshouse's most experienced man—the **gaffer**. He went to his bench near the furnace and sat down with the punty laid across the bench's iron arms.

The gaffer hung his tools on hooks along the edges of his wooden bench. He had shears of different sizes and shapes. He used some shears to squeeze sections of the bubble to produce the narrow neck of a bottle. Others were especially sharp and used for clipping off rough edges. The gaffer might reach for metal tongs or tweezers to flatten and pull at sections of the glass. He rolled the punty as he worked so that gravity would not cause the bubble to fall. When necessary, he passed the glass to a nearby assistant to be reheated. In the gaffer's hands the bubble slowly turned into a delicate wineglass, bowl, or dish. It was a slow process requiring the highest levels of patience, skill, and creative flair.

*The gaffer rolls a parison of glass on the punty and shapes it with metal tongs.*

## Extra Touches

The glassmaker could sell the gaffer's finished product as it was or could pass it on to another craftsman to be decorated. The workers sometimes **gilded** fine glass, or painted it with gold. Other times they used a sharp flint needle to engrave letters or a design on the object's surface. Glass cutters created textures by placing the glass against a spinning metal or stone wheel, which carved away sections to create a chosen pattern.

The glassblower could also produce decorated glass by blowing it into a mold. He hired a woodcarver to make the first mold, which showed the shape of the object—for example, a wine bottle or a cream pitcher. The wooden mold also bore the pattern that would appear on the glass. Parallel grooved lines, flowers, and diamonds were popular among colonists. Another worker made a metal mold from the original one. Convenient hinges allowed workers to open and close this second mold. It had no lid, so the glassblower could insert a parison. He blew the glass until a bubble filled the mold. After he removed the glass, he could blow it more to make the object larger. The molded pattern would remain perfect as it stretched.

Colonists were also drawn to colorful glass. Iron and nickel, which occurred naturally in the sand, gave glass a warm green

# A Risky Job

Glassworkers knew their jobs were dangerous. They could expect to get burns from contact with the scalding furnaces and glass. They also risked inhaling hot air while blowing a parison. Workers suffered lung damage from years of exposure to sand and flint. The dust from these materials was constantly in the air of the glasshouse. Tiny, sharp fragments became lodged in the workers' lungs and caused workers to cough and become short of breath. To reduce this risk, the glasshouse was closed for several months each year. But time took its toll on the workers' health.

Some of the chemicals used in glassmaking also threatened the health of glassworkers. Exposure to lead, which was added to flint glass to improve melting, could harm a worker's hearing, vision, muscle coordination, kidneys, lungs, and more. However, because the symptoms of lead poisoning are easily confused with those of other diseases, many glassblowers may have suffered significant health problems without knowing the cause. Another dangerous substance was arsenic, which glassblowers sometimes used to make glass more colorful and brilliant. Low exposure to arsenic caused discoloration of the skin and warts. High exposure affected the nervous system and may have caused lung cancer. Glassblowing was an important job, but it came with a price.

color. A glassmaker could add small amounts of other metals to the frit to alter this shade. For example, he added cobalt to the mix to make blue glass. Gold made the glass red, and manganese turned it purple.

Whether they produced practical items or stunning decorative objects, the colonial glassblower and his team could be proud. They made products that colonists would enjoy for years to come.

## Independence

In the eighteenth century there were few glass craftsmen in the colonies, and they could not satisfy the increasing demand for glass. Many shops continued to sell imported glass to make up the difference. But the success of colonial glassblowers made their English competitors nervous.

The royal government was not pleased with the colonial glassblowers' success, either. England relied heavily on the money colonists spent on imported goods. In the mid-1760s England was also in debt after fighting the French and Indian War to obtain new land west of its original colonies. In an effort to offset the war debt through extra revenue from the colonies, the British Parliament began taxing imported goods, including glass and lead.

The plan backfired. Colonists protested that the tax law was unconstitutional because the English government wrote it without an elected colonial representative present to look after colonists' rights. The colonists immediately stopped buying English goods. Instead they purchased goods from local craftsmen. At the time, Henry William Stiegel was one of colonies' two major glassmakers. At his glasshouse in Pennsylvania, Stiegel responded to the situation with gusto. Within a short time his factory offered a selection of glass as diverse and well made as that from England.

Parliament eventually cancelled the tax, but the damage had been done. This was only one of many events that created mistrust and frustration between the English and groups of colonists who were ready for independence. Colonial patriots began to discuss the idea of a revolution. In 1775 British and colonial troops fought the first battle of the American Revolution in Boston. Colonists declared their independence a year later, but they would continue to fight the English until 1783.

Under English rule colonists had not been allowed to move west into land gained during the French and Indian War. After the American Revolution this land was wide open for settlement. The United States of America stretched from the Atlantic Ocean

*Like many other colonists, after the American Revolution some glassblowers loaded up their wagons and moved to newly opened U.S. territory in the West.*

to the Mississippi River. By 1803 it would include land as far west as the Rocky Mountains. Glassblowers were among the settlers who spread across the countryside. They sought new locations that could provide the materials needed to make glass.

Just thirty years after the war, there were forty-four glasshouses in the United States. The glass industry got a major boost in the 1820s, when government officials added taxes on imported goods. Americans could save as much as 40 percent by purchasing local glass. Around the same time, inventors introduced machines that molded glass. Now more glass could be produced in less time. Mass production also made glass more affordable. The glass-blower's work was no longer reserved for the wealthy. It could bring touches of elegance to the lives of average Americans.

# Glossary

| | |
|---|---|
| *annealing* | cooling slowly |
| *apprenticeship* | an agreement whereby a person works with an expert to learn a new skill or job |
| *blowing rod* | a metal tube used to pick up and blow hot glass |
| *craftsmen* | trained workers who make objects by hand |
| *crucibles* | large, heat-resistant pots |
| *flint glass* | heavy glass that is used in lenses and prisms |
| *frit* | the mixture of ingredients from which glass is made |
| *gaffer* | the most experienced, or head, glassblower |
| *gilded* | painted with a thin layer of gold |
| *glasshouse* | a factory in which glass is made |
| *imported* | purchased and moved something from another country |
| *kiln* | a specialized oven used to fire clay |
| *lehr* | an oven that is designed to anneal glass |
| *lime* | a form of calcium that is found in seashells |
| *marver* | a glassblower's table, used to smooth glass as it is worked |
| *parison* | a ball of hot glass |
| *potash* | a substance produced from the ashes of burned wood |
| *potters* | craftsmen who make clay containers |

| | |
|---|---|
| *punty* | an iron rod used to hold glass as it is worked |
| *ration* | to give out food or other supplies in small amounts |
| *soda ash* | a substance produced from the ashes of burned seaweed |
| *tableware* | items used to serve food |

# *Find Out More*

## BOOKS

Fishkin, Rebecca Love. *English Colonies in America*. Mankato, MN: Compass Point Books, 2008.

Kalman, Bobbie. *A Visual Dictionary of a Colonial Community*. New York: Crabtree Publishing Company, 2008.

Landau, Elaine. *Explore Jamestown with Elaine Landau*. Berkeley Heights, NJ: Enslow Elementary, 2006.

Winters, Kay. *Colonial Voices: Hear Them Speak*. New York: Dutton Juvenile, 2008.

# WEBSITES

### Colonial Williamsburg Kids Zone

www.history.org/kids/

Tour the colonial capital of Virginia and meet some of its important residents. This site offers games, activities, and resources about colonial life and history.

### Glass Chemistry Game (Corning Museum of Glass)

www.cmog.org/glasschemistry/

This site offers an entertaining and informative video and an interactive game to expand your knowledge about the chemical composition of glass.

### Jamestown Glasshouse

www.nps.gov/jame/planyourvisit/glasshouse.htm

Jamestown has been re-created within a U.S. national park. This site describes the glasshouse and provides information about visiting the park.

### Museum of Glass

www.museumofglass.org/education/learn-about-glass/glassblowing/

Learn about modern glassblowing on this site from the glass museum in Tacoma, Washington.

# Index

Page numbers in **boldface** are illustrations.

## About the Author

Christine Petersen has written more than three dozen books and several magazine articles for a variety of audiences, from emerging readers to adults. Her subjects include science, nature, and social studies. When she's not writing, Petersen and her young son enjoy exploring the natural areas near their home in Minneapolis, Minnesota. Petersen is a member of the Society of Children's Book Writers and Illustrators.